WORLD WAR I

Remembering
the Great War

THE UNITED STATES IN WORLD WAR I

America's Entry Ensures Victory

JANE H. GOULD

Crabtree Publishing Company

www.crabtreebooks.com

WORLD WAR I

Remembering the Great War

Author: Jane H. Gould
Editor: Lynn Peppas
Proofreaders: Lisa Slone, Wendy Scavuzzo
Editorial director: Kathy Middleton
Production coordinator: Shivi Sharma
Design concept: Margaret Amy Salter
Cover design: Ken Wright
Photo research: Nivisha Sinha, Crystal Sikkens
Maps: Contentra Technologies
**Production coordinator and
     Prepress technician:** Tammy McGarr
Print coordinator: Katherine Berti

Written, developed, and produced by
     Contentra Technologies

Cover: A poster supporting American troops
     fighting in World War I
Title page: President Woodrow Wilson asking
     Congress to declare war on Germany,
     April 2, 1917
Contents page: Wilson-Marshall Campaign
     Buttons and Inaugural Badge

Photo Credits:
Alamy: Content Page (© Bygone Collection), 12 (© The Art Archive), 16b (© The
     Print Collector), 23 (© SOTK2011), 30 (Chronicle), 31 (© The Print Collector),
     33 (© Classic Image), 34 (© Maurice Savage), 36 (© Ivy Close Images),
     38b (© Folio), 40 (© akg-images), 41 (Chronicle), 44 (© Burton Holmes
     Historical Collection)
The Bridgeman Art Library: 6 (European immigrants passing the Statue of Liberty in
     New York Harbour, 1892 (coloured engraving), American School, (19th century)/
     Private Collection/Peter Newark American Pictures), 11 (Where are your Ships?
     illustration from a German magazine, 'Simplicissimus', c. 1915 (litho), Thony,
     Eduard (1866–1950)/Private Collection/The Stapleton Collection)
Corbis: 13 (© Bettmann), 18t, 42
DOD Media: 39
Getty Images: 35 (UIG via Getty Images),
Library of Congress: 8 (LC-USZC4-10878), 14 (LC-USZC4-13285), 15 (LC-DIG-ds-
     03216), 16t (LC-USZC4-10881), 18b (LC-USZ62-9981), 20t (LC-USZ62-8422),
     20b (LC-USZC4-10297), 22 (LC-DIG-hec-06197), 24t (LC-DIG-ggbain-24173),
     24b (LC-USZC4-10333), 25 (LC-USZ62-67912), 26 (LC-USZ62-111143),
     27 (LC-USZC4-5855), 29 (LC-DIG-ggbain-24969)
National Archives and Records Administration: 19, 38t (Records of the War
     Department General and Special. Staffs)
Wikipedia: 7 (Official White House portrait of Woodrow Wilson)
Cover: The Granger Collection, NYC
Title Page: Library of Congress (LC-USZC4-10297)
Back cover: Wikimedia Commons: Library and Archives Canada (background)
     Shutterstock: I. Pilon (medals); Shuttertock: IanC66 (airplane)

t=Top, b=Bottom, l=Left, r=Right

Library and Archives Canada Cataloguing in Publication

Gould, Jane H., 1956-, author
     The United States in World War I : America's entry ensures victory
/ Jane H. Gould.

(World War I : remembering the Great War)
Includes index.
Issued in print and electronic formats.
ISBN 978-0-7787-0389-1 (bound).--ISBN 978-0-7787-0395-2 (pbk.).--
ISBN 978-1-4271-7507-6 (pdf).--ISBN 978-1-4271-7501-4 (html)

     1. World War, 1914-1918--United States--Juvenile literature.
2. United States--History--1913-1921--Juvenile literature. I. Title.

D570.G68 2014   j940.4'0973   C2014-903264-1
                                            C2014-903265-X

Library of Congress Cataloging-in-Publication Data

Gould, Jane H.
 The United States in World War I : America's entry ensures victory / Jane
H. Gould.
     pages cm. -- (World War I : remembering the Great War)
 Includes index.
 Audience: Ages 10-13.
 ISBN 978-0-7787-0389-1 (reinforced library binding : alk. paper) -- ISBN
978-0-7787-0395-2 (pbk. : alk. paper) -- ISBN 978-1-4271-7507-6 (electronic
pdf : alk. paper) -- ISBN 978-1-4271-7501-4 (electronic html : alk. paper)
1. World War, 1914-1918--Campaigns--Juvenile literature. I. Title.

 D522.7.G68 2014
 940.4'0973--dc23

                                        2014017862

Crabtree Publishing Company

www.crabtreebooks.com   1-800-387-7650

Printed in Canada/052014/MA20140505

Published in Canada
Crabtree Publishing
616 Welland Ave.
St. Catharines, Ontario
L2M 5V6

Published in the United States
Crabtree Publishing
PMB 59051
350 Fifth Avenue, 59th Floor
New York, New York 10118

Published in the United Kingdom
Crabtree Publishing
Maritime House
Basin Road North, Hove
BN41 1WR

Published in Australia
Crabtree Publishing
3 Charles Street
Coburg North
VIC, 3058

CONTENTS

THE U.S. JOINS THE ALLIES

On June 28, a Bosnian-Serb **assassinated** the archduke of the Austro-Hungarian Empire. Austria-Hungary responded by declaring war on Serbia. This act launched Europe and the world into war. A series of **alliances** caused the major powers of Europe to choose sides. Russia supported Serbia. France, Britain, and Russia formed the Allied forces. Germany and Austria-Hungary formed the Central Powers. When World War I began in August 1914, the warring nations did not think it would last long. Soon, though, many other countries were caught up in the war. Fighting spread throughout Europe, the Middle East, and as far away as Africa and China.

By the time the United States joined the conflict in April 1917, the war seemed as though it would never end. On the Western Front, Germany and the Allies were stuck in a **stalemate**. Trench warfare made it impossible for anyone to win. The armies of both sides were exhausted. They were short of soldiers, supplies, and money. The people in these countries were angry about the terrible loss of life and the hardships they had to suffer. On the Eastern Front, the Russian citizens had revolted, and other governments were falling.

The U.S. did not want to get involved in a European war. For the first two years, the nation stayed **neutral**. As the war continued, though, it began to affect Americans more and more. When the United States finally declared war on Germany, it gave new hope to the Allied cause and helped turn the fight around.

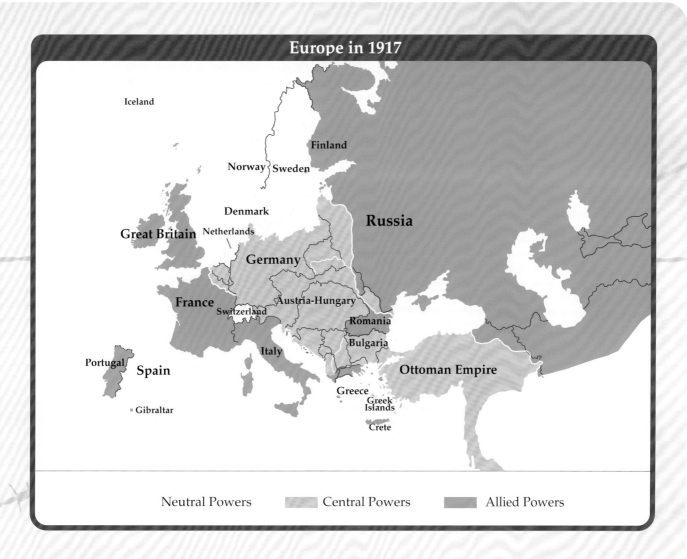

Europe in 1917

Neutral Powers   Central Powers   Allied Powers

EUROPE IN 1917

As shown in the map above, the Central Powers included Germany, Austria-Hungary, and the Ottoman Empire. Bulgaria had joined their ranks in 1915, and by 1917, the Central Powers were occupying the neutral countries of Belgium and Luxembourg, as well as Serbia, Montenegro, and most of Romania.

The Allied Powers included Great Britain, France, Russia, Portugal, Italy, and parts of Greece.

Taking and holding new territory had become extremely costly for both sides. It would take the entry of the United States and the withdrawal of Russia in 1917 to push the war toward its outcome.

CHAPTER 1

WORLD WAR I BEGINS

Major Events

1914

June 28
A Bosnian-Serb assassinates Archduke Franz Ferdinand of Austria-Hungary.

July 28
Austria-Hungary declares war on Serbia.

August 1
Germany declares war on Russia.

August 4
Germany invades Belgium.

1915

February 14
Germany begins submarine warfare.

May 7
The *Lusitania* is sunk by a German U-boat.

1916

April 19
President Wilson issues a warning to Germany.

November 7
President Wilson is re-elected.

1917

February 1
Germany starts unrestricted U-boat attacks.

February 3
The U.S. ends relations with Germany.

February 24
President Wilson sees the Zimmermann telegram.

After Austria-Hungary declared war on Serbia on July 28, 1914, European countries quickly took sides in the conflict. Russia, France, and Britain became the Allied forces. Germany joined with Austria-Hungary to form the Central Powers. Within months, the war had spread to countries around the world. The United States, however, would not get drawn in at that time.

AMERICA STAYS NEUTRAL

Woodrow Wilson was president of the United States when war broke out in Europe. He declared the United States a neutral country. That meant that America would not fight. It would not side with either the Allies or the Central Powers. Most American citizens agreed with their president. They thought the war was Europe's problem, not theirs.

RIGHT: *America was made up of **immigrants** from all countries involved in World War 1.*

America in 1914

Many changes were going on in the United States in 1914. The economy was in a **recession**, or slump. Times were hard for many Americans. New factories were being built, but many people still had trouble finding work, and workers were often not treated fairly.

Many immigrants came from other countries to live in the United States. They moved to make their lives better or escape from troubles in their own countries. From 1907 to 1917, over 650,000 immigrants came to the U.S. every year. In the early 1900s, about one-third of all Americans had recently immigrated or had a parent who had immigrated.

Since there was more industrial work in large cities, many of the immigrants lived there. Americans were also moving from **rural** to **urban** areas. People left small towns and farms. African-Americans came north. The new arrivals often lived in poor and crowded conditions.

New technology also changed life for many people. Cars, telephones, and electric lights were slowly becoming more common. Communication and travel were faster and easier. The days of horses and gas lamps were coming to an end.

WOODROW WILSON (1856–1924)

Woodrow Wilson was the 28th president of the United States. He served two terms, from 1913–1921.

Although Wilson could not keep America out of World War I, he tried to lead the world into a long-lasting peace. In January 1918, he presented Congress with his "Fourteen Points." They included ways to make the world "fit and safe to live in," including a League of Nations that would settle international **disputes** peacefully. The Fourteen Points were eventually included in the Treaty of Versailles, which officially ended the war.

Divided Europe, Divided America

Americans weren't sure whom to support when Europe split into the Allies and Central Powers. President Wilson was a **pacifist**, who thought peace was worth any price. He wanted to avoid fighting and stay friendly with both sides.

Europe had been in many wars, and most Americans wanted to stay out of this new one. Still, different groups had different loyalties. Many Americans had British ancestors, so they supported Britain and the Allies. There was also a lot of sympathy for the French, because they had helped the United States in the Revolutionary War.

On the other hand, there were also millions of immigrants who felt closer to the Central Powers. Their families were from Germany, Austria-Hungary, or the Balkans. The Irish also thought of Britain as their enemy; they had been fighting each other for centuries.

RIGHT: *Posters such as this encouraged men to enlist in the military.*

WHAT DO YOU THINK?
How was the United States involved in the war while it was neutral?

THE "SCRAP OF PAPER"

These are the signatures and seals of the representatives of the Six Powers to the "Scrap of Paper"—the Treaty signed in 1839 guaranteeing the independence and neutrality of Belgium.
"Palmerston" signed for Britain. "Bülow" for Prussia.

The Germans have broken their pledged word and devastated Belgium. Help to keep your Country's honour bright by restoring Belgium her liberty.

ENLIST TO-DAY

AMERICA MOVES TOWARD WAR

The European powers turned to other countries for supplies, such as weapons, materials, food, and other resources they needed to wage war. The Allies and the Central Powers both turned to the United States.

Boost to the Economy

The United States wanted to stay out of the conflict. However, it decided that it would trade with Britain, Germany, and other nations in the war. It also allowed its banks and businesses to lend money to these countries.

Both sides borrowed money to buy supplies. They ordered food from American farms and war materials from its factories. The U.S. economy began to get better. Factories were **manufacturing** weapons, clothing, and vehicles. More people were working. America sent billions of dollars of supplies to Britain and France. Germany received almost $400 million of goods.

WHAT DO YOU KNOW?

AMERICAN LOANS

During the war, European countries had to buy many supplies from the United States. However, they needed their own money to fight. So American bankers loaned them money to pay for the supplies.

These loans were a problem for President Wilson. Since America was neutral, he only wanted to loan money to other neutral countries. Lending to warring nations could show that the U.S. favored one side over the other. Eventually, Wilson allowed bankers to give loans to either side. He was concerned that not doing so could damage America's economy during the war.

The British Blockade

When the war started, everyone thought it would end quickly. The battles on the Western Front soon became stalemates, where neither side could win. More countries entered the fight, and there were more fronts to supply. As the conflict dragged on, the warring sides began running out of food, fuel, ammunition, and other important resources.

The British Naval Blockade of Germany

Legend:
- Northern patrol and mines
- Naval war zone declared by Germany in 1915
- Dover patrol and mines

Americans could trade with the Central Powers, but it was difficult. Britain had set up a naval **blockade** around Germany. British warships stopped any vessels with materials going to the Germans. Even though American ships were neutral, they were searched. If they found any goods that could help Germany, the British took them, and the ship was turned back.

Many Americans were unhappy with Britain when its navy seized American ships. However, Britain controlled the seas. They also wouldn't buy from U.S. companies that did business with Germany. Soon, most American trade was with the Allies. U.S. businesses sent money and supplies to them. This created stronger support for the Allied cause.

Germans saw that the United States was sending more aid to the Allies. They began to question America's neutral stance. The Germans decided to start their own blockade. Their navy was not as strong as the British navy. However, they had U-boats.

WHAT DO YOU THINK?
Why did Americans want to side with the Allies rather than the Central Powers?

German U-Boats

In German, submarines are called *unterseebooten* (undersea boats). In English, they were called U-boats. At the beginning of the war, Germany had only thirty-eight submarines. By the end of the war there were over 300 on the seas.

German ships could not leave their ports because the British had ringed the area with explosive mines. In sea battles, their regular warships had lost against the British navy. U-boats, however, could slip through the mine fields. They could surprise ships and sink them with torpedoes. The Germans decided U-boats would be more helpful than warships in fighting back against the British blockade.

LEFT: *German U-boat on patrol*

The German Blockade In February 1915, Germany declared the waters around Britain a war zone. They said they would begin **unrestricted** submarine warfare. That meant they would attack any ship that entered that area, even if it was from a neutral country. If a U-boat commander thought the ship carried supplies for the Allies, he could fire a torpedo. It was expected that submarine commanders would warn **merchant** ships before firing on them. They would allow civilian sailors to get into the lifeboats. Then they would sink the ship. In unrestricted warfare, German submarines began firing without warning.

Germany said it would end the submarine attacks if Britain would allow food and raw materials through. Britain agreed to allow food through. Raw materials, though, could help Germany in the war, so the British refused to let ships carrying raw materials through.

The First U-Boat Attacks The Central Powers worried that the U.S. would enter the war if its ships were attacked. Despite that, Germany began targeting vessels from neutral countries.

On February 19, a U-boat sank a Norwegian oil tanker.

BELOW: *The RMS Falaba, a British cargo-passenger ship, was torpedoed and sunk by a German U-boat on March 28, 1915.*

On May 1, an American **merchant** ship, the *Gulflight*, was torpedoed. President Wilson was angry. He warned the Germans that America would not put up with attacks on American citizens or ships. Germany offered to pay for the *Gulflight*. However, the Germans did not stop their U-boat policy. The blockade was causing Germany many problems. Many supplies were growing short, especially food. Germany felt that stopping the blockade was worth the risk of angering the United States.

THE SINKING OF THE *LUSITANIA*

The *Lusitania* was a British passenger ship. It was one of the fastest, largest, and most luxurious ships to sail the Atlantic. On May 1, 1915, it left New York to sail to England.

There were 1,959 passengers on the ship, including many U.S. citizens. There was also a load of **munitions** on board, which could be used for Allied weapons. On the day it sailed, Germany put an ad in New York newspapers. It warned passengers that they traveled at their own risk. Few people canceled.

A U-Boat Strikes

On May 7, the *Lusitania* reached the coast of Ireland. The captain, William Turner, had not been warned that a U-boat had sunk two British ships in that area the day before. Submarines had a hard time aiming at ships that zigzagged. Captain Turner thought it was a waste of fuel and time though, so he **refrained**.

ABOVE: *The Lusitania under attack*

In early afternoon, a lookout saw a trail of bubbles heading toward the *Lusitania*. He sounded an alarm, but it was too late. A torpedo from a U-boat tore a hole in the ship. Passengers heard two explosions. It took less than 20 minutes for the *Lusitania* to sink. Even though there were enough lifeboats, they couldn't be launched properly.

A total of 1,198 passengers and crew members, including 128 American men, women, and children, were killed. News of the disaster was quickly picked up around the world. People were horrified and outraged by the deaths of so many innocent people.

American Reaction

In the United States, newspapers called the sinking "deliberate murder." They believed that Germany had planned to sink the *Lusitania* in advance. Many politicians called for war with Germany. There were anti-German **demonstrations** around the country. President Wilson sent four angry protests to Germany, stating that Germany's actions were "unlawful and **inhuman**."

Germany defended itself by saying that the *Lusitania* was carrying war materials. They were angry that Britain was not being punished for causing innocent Germans to starve. They also believed that Britain had used the *Lusitania's* passengers to keep the ship from being attacked.

President Wilson and the American public did not listen to those arguments. They did not ask Britain to end its blockade. Instead, the United States blamed Germany for its U-boat attacks. Germany agreed to no longer fire at ships without warning.

Despite the country's anger, President Wilson still would not go to war. On May 10, he gave a speech saying that America would remain neutral. Many Americans still agreed with him.

WHAT DO YOU THINK?
What is propaganda? Why might it cause problems?

RIGHT: *British posters relied heavily on propaganda to stir up anti-German sentiments.*

AMERICANS TURN TOWARD THE ALLIES

The British used **propaganda** to play up German **brutality**. Newspaper cartoons, posters, and postcards made the Central Powers look as evil as possible. The Germans also created their own propaganda. However, they were unable to get much of it out to the world.

DESTROY THIS MAD BRUTE

ENLIST

Anti-German Propaganda

Even before the *Lusitania* was sunk, Americans heard about terrible acts done by German soldiers. When Germany invaded Belgium, there were stories about Germans shooting babies and innocent townspeople. Women were attacked and young men were tortured.

This propaganda was often untrue or very **exaggerated**. It was used to make Americans hate the Germans and think of them as the enemy. The Allies were often shown as heroes or saintly victims. Germans were drawn to look like monsters. They were called names like "beasts" or "Huns."

In October 1915, a British nurse named Edith Cavell was arrested in Belgium by the Germans. She had cared for both Allied and German soldiers. However, she had also helped many Allied soldiers escape from the German army. The German military decided that what she had done was a crime. They gave her the death sentence.

People from around the world protested, including Germans. On October 12, Cavell was shot by a firing squad. Her death caused strong feelings of outrage in Britain and in many neutral countries. The British used it as anti-German propaganda. Artists created scenes of her arrest, trial, and execution. In America and elsewhere, she became a **martyr**.

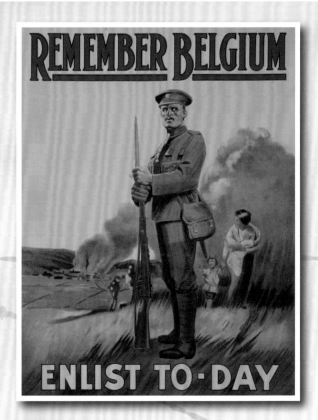

ABOVE: *Posters like this one proved to be an effective tool in encouraging men to enlist.*

RIGHT: *Edith Cavell (1865–1915)*

U-boat Attacks on American Ships, 1915–1916

Eleven American ships were sunk or damaged by U-boats between 1915 and 1916. Not all locations are known. By the end of the war, a total of 174 American ships had been sunk or damaged.

Leelanau - July 25, 1915 ★

Norway

Denmark

Great Britain

Seaconnet - June 18, 1916 ★

Netherlands

Germany

Galena - November 24, 1916 ★

Belgium

Luxembourg

Nebraskan - May 25, 1915 ★

Lusitania* - May 7, 1915 ★

France

Switzerland

Italy

Columbian - November 8, 1916 ★

Spain

Portugal

Lanao - October 28, 1916 ★

Chemung - November 26, 1916 ★

Morocco

Algeria

Tunisia

★ Location of American ship sunk or damaged by U-boats.
* Note: The *Lusitania* was not an American ship.

Early Volunteers

More people in the United States threw their support behind the Allies. They began to believe that Germany wanted to destroy freedom and democracy. Most Americans felt they had to help save the world from the evil Central Powers.

Many took action without waiting for their country. U.S. organizations raised money for war refugees and wounded Allied soldiers. Almost 15,000 American men joined armies in Canada, Britain, and France so that they could fight. Women volunteered as nurses and doctors in England, France, Russia, and Serbia. Both men and women worked as ambulance drivers on the war fronts.

AMERICA DECIDES

In March 1916, a U-boat attacked the *Sussex*, a British passenger ship. Eighty people were killed, including two Americans. The next month, President Wilson warned Germany that America would end its relations if submarines continued to attack passenger and merchant vessels. The Germans again promised not to attack without warning.

Wilson Is Re-elected

Americans were still very divided during the presidential elections. Many were ready to declare war. They wanted to help the Allies. Others felt very strongly about supporting peace efforts. Wilson's campaign **slogan** was "He kept us out of war." On November 7, 1916, Wilson won a very close election.

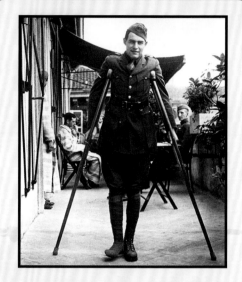

AMBULANCE DRIVERS

When the war began, France had very few motorized ambulances. Organizations or wealthy Americans sent over donated cars that were **modified** to carry wounded soldiers. Few people drove cars in the early 1900s, so many of the volunteer ambulance drivers came from families that could afford a vehicle. A number of American drivers later became famous, including Walt Disney and writer Ernest Hemingway, shown above.

Opening game 1916.   Bx 112

ABOVE: *A smiling Woodrow Wilson threw the first pitch on baseball's opening day in 1916.*

Germany Goes on the Offense

In Europe, the Battles of Verdun and the Somme had raged through much of 1916. Millions were killed or wounded, yet trench warfare kept both sides from advancing.

The Germans decided that the best way to defeat Britain was at sea. German attacks destroyed needed supplies, and the British were suffering. In January 1917, they renewed their unrestricted U-boat attacks. This included American vessels in British waters. On February 3, President Wilson broke off diplomatic relations with Germany.

The Germans believed that if the United States entered the war, Germany's chances of winning would be very poor. Germany continued its submarine warfare. If they could defeat Britain quickly, they could then crush France. In March, German U-boats sank four American vessels.

RIGHT: *The Zimmermann telegram was written in a secret code.*

WHAT DO YOU THINK?
Why didn't Germany believe that the United States would be a threat?

The Zimmermann Telegram

In January 1917, a German diplomat named Arthur Zimmermann sent a **telegram** to the president of Mexico. The note asked Mexico to join the Central Powers. In return, Mexico would get back the land that it had lost to America. That included Texas, New Mexico, and Arizona.

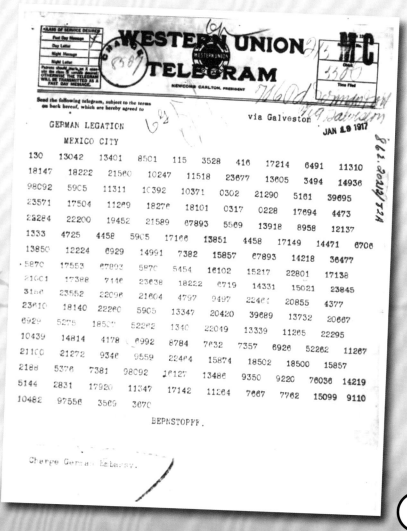

19

The British got hold of the telegram and decoded it. In February, they sent it to the U.S. government. On March 1, President Wilson told the American press about the note. Americans were furious with Germany's actions. They thought Germany was insulting the United States. People marched in support of a war.

War Is Declared

On April 2, 1917, President Wilson made a powerful speech to Congress. He said that the United States had no choice. It was its duty to fight so the world could be "made safe for democracy." After the speech, he returned to the White House and cried. He did not want to send young men into battle.

Four days later, both the House and Senate voted for the war.

JEANNETTE RANKIN (1880–1973)

When Congress voted to go to war, one member who voted "no" was Jeannette Rankin. Rankin was the first woman in Congress. When her state of Montana granted women the right to vote in 1914, she ran for office. She won the election to the House of Representatives in 1916. When she voted against the war, many people in Montana were furious. She was not re-elected. However, in 1940 she again won a seat in the House. In 1941, she voted against entering World War II— the only politician who voted to stay out of both world wars.

LEFT: *President Wilson asked Congress to declare war on Germany and to join the Allies.*

CHAPTER 2

THE U.S. ENTERS THE WAR

When the United States entered the war, many Americans celebrated. Thousands of young men volunteered for military service. There was a great burst of patriotic spirit. American songwriter George M. Cohan composed a catchy song called *Over There*, which proclaimed that "the Yanks are coming" to end the war. It soon became a big hit.

The Allies were also overjoyed. Britain and France sent people to Washington asking for immediate help. They were disappointed, though, to find that America was not ready to send more troops or supplies.

Major Events
1917

April 6
America declares war on Germany.

April 13
Committee on Public Information is formed.

May 18
Selective Service begins.

December 7
America declares war on Austria-Hungary.

AMERICA PREPARES TO FIGHT

Even though American citizens were eager to "save" the Allies, the government wasn't prepared. President Wilson had done little to raise and train an army while the country was neutral. The United States had few trained troops or experienced officers. There were no camps where they could train a large army. The Food Administration was established to ration food, so that more could be sent overseas for the troops. Weapons, ammunition, and war materials were in short supply. The Allies were relieved to have America's help, but they were unhappy that they would have to wait.

WHAT DO YOU THINK?
Why couldn't America send an army to Europe as soon as it joined the war?

Building an Army

Many volunteers joined the army, navy, and marines. However, it was not enough, and more soldiers were needed quickly. In May 1917, President Wilson signed the Selective Service Act. This allowed the government to **draft** men into the army. While it originally targeted men 21 to 30 years of age, the draft was later expanded to include men between 18 and 45 who were fit enough to fight.

ABOVE: *Officers at a training camp in Plattsburgh, New York*

All males in that age group had to **register** and were given a **lottery** number. If their number was called, they were checked to see if they were fit to fight. Many were not accepted. Others refused to serve or did not show up when they were called. Millions of men registered, but the number of actual army **recruits** was much smaller.

The new soldiers, called "doughboys," came from a wide range of citizens. There were immigrants who didn't speak English well. Young farmers came from remote areas where no one had ever seen a city or even a large town. Many were uneducated. Almost one quarter of the recruits couldn't read or even sign their names.

WHAT DO YOU KNOW?

DOUGHBOYS

No one is sure where the term "doughboys" came from. It had been used in earlier wars, but came to be an affectionate nickname for the American men who fought in World War I. Some say it came about from the doughy biscuits soldiers ate. Another theory compares their large uniform buttons to a type of popular doughnut. "Doughboy" might even be a play on the word "adobe." During the Mexican-American War (1846–1848), soldiers frequently were covered with white **adobe** dust from shelling Mexican homes.

ABOVE: *New soldiers received rigorous training with guns and bayonets.*

At the start of 1917, the army had just over 100,000 men. By September, about half a million recruits were ready to start training. By the end of the war, some 4 million troops were fighting or ready for combat.

Preparing the Troops

Once the army got soldiers, they needed to be trained, housed, and equipped. Within a few months, hundreds of thousands of workmen had built training camps for 1.5 million men. Instructors had to be hired to teach the men. Recruits learned military skills but had other schooling, too. Camps taught classes in English, American culture, and other subjects.

THE COMMITTEE OF PUBLIC INFORMATION

The U.S. government wanted to make sure American citizens supported the war. It created the Committee of Public Information (CPI) to get news out to the public. The man in charge of the CPI was George Creel. He hired writers, artists, and entertainers to "sell the war."

Soon the CPI was creating propaganda in the form of posters, booklets, advertisements, and even movies. It was used to promote patriotism and make people hate the Germans. Citizens were encouraged to join the military, work in factories, buy **bonds**, and conserve food.

The CPI also sent people to give short speeches at movie theaters. These "Four-Minute Men" (and women) would talk about the war during intermissions. Usually they focused on a topic that Creel thought needed support. Soon the speeches were being given in churches, synagogues, clubs, and other gathering places. There were Four-Minute Men who spoke to immigrants in their native languages.

Liberty Bonds

One of the CPI's most important goals was selling Liberty Bonds. The war cost millions of dollars every day. Liberty Bonds were a way for the government to raise money. Starting in June 1917, Americans started buying bonds, which cost a few dollars. Bond rallies were held all over the country. Famous movie stars such as Charlie Chaplin performed and spoke at the rallies. By the end of the war, over $21 billion dollars in bonds were sold.

**GEORGE CREEL
(1876–1953)**

George Creel was a journalist and newspaper publisher. He was a supporter of Woodrow Wilson. Once Creel became chairman of the CPI, he carried out his work with great enthusiasm and creativity. He used his position to spread Wilson's views throughout the U.S. and even around the world. To make sure he got public support, his committee issued daily pro-war press releases from the government. The CPI gave away millions of propaganda pamphlets in different languages. After the war, Creel continued to work for Wilson in support of his Fourteen Points.

LEFT: *Special appeals were made to women, encouraging them to buy Liberty Bonds.*

ABOVE: *Charlie Chaplin, Mary Pickford, and other movie stars went to Washington to help sell Liberty Bonds.*

Anti-German Hysteria

George Creel's propaganda campaign was very successful. However, it also had a very ugly side. People who did not support the war or refused to fight were in danger. They were considered unpatriotic and were often **harassed** or even beaten.

German Americans were also targets. They were as loyal as other American citizens, and many were in the U.S. Army. Many, though, spoke German or enjoyed German culture. Americans became suspicious of anything German. Some schools stopped teaching the language. German music wasn't played. Even the names of German foods were changed. Sauerkraut was called "liberty cabbage," and hamburgers were called "salisbury steak."

People sometimes got fired up by the anti-German propaganda. Suspicions became so great that neighbors or coworkers turned against innocent people. Germans were accused of being spies. They could be arrested for no reason. Worse, there were attacks on Germans. Some were even killed by mobs. To stay safe, some people with German names changed them.

The patriotic spirit that brought people together also, dangerously, left many people out.

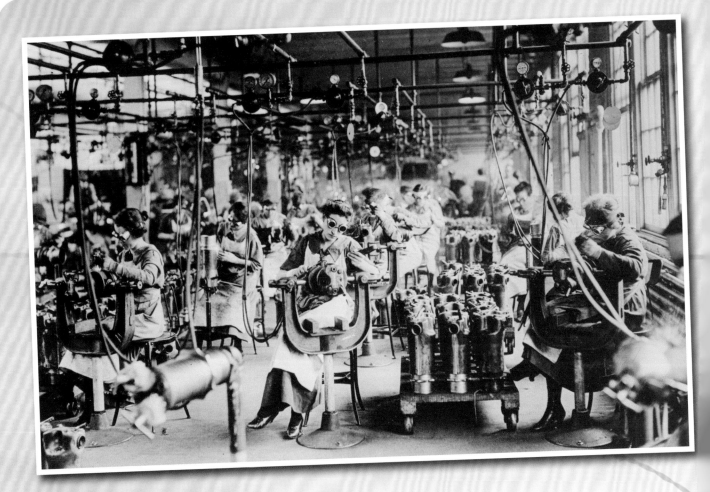

ABOVE: *Women took jobs that they had never held before, including working in factories as welders.*

THE WAR AT HOME

The war provided many new jobs and increased production. Once again, America's economy started to thrive. A government office called the War Industries Board decided what war supplies were needed. It found businesses that could provide these goods.

The United States needed to have enough equipment for their own troops and for the Allies. Factories quickly went to work making uniforms, tents, weapons, ammunition, and many other supplies. New naval and merchant ships were built.

As more men were drafted, many women took their places in the factories. For the first time, women were given the same pay and jobs as men.

THE
WOMAN'S LAND ARMY
of AMERICA

TRAINING   SCHOOL
UNIVERSITY of VIRGINIA
JUNE 15 TO SEPTEMBER 15 • COURSES TWO WEEKS
TUITION FREE • BOARD $5.00 PER WEEK
Apply WOMAN'S LAND ARMY, U. S. EMPLOYMENT SERVICE, 910 E. Main Street, RICHMOND, VA

ABOVE: *Women took active roles during wartime, working on farms and in factories.*

Rationing

Americans also needed to ration, or use less, food and fuel. These needed to be saved for the troops, as well as for the Allies. More food had to be grown, too. Men and women left towns to work on farms. Food production went up 25 percent.

Since wheat and meat were sent overseas, families pledged to stick to a controlled diet. There were "wheatless Mondays" and "meatless Tuesdays," and other ways to conserve at every meal. People ate oatmeal and coarse **Victory bread**. They grew their own fruit and vegetables in Victory Gardens. Energy use was also cut with personal sacrifices such as "heatless Mondays" and "gasless Sundays."

CHAPTER 3

THE YANKS ARE COMING

The United States' army in Europe was called the American Expeditionary Force (AEF). Its commander was General John "Black Jack" Pershing.

Pershing did not want to continue the strategy of trench warfare. He believed that the Americans could end the stalemate with full-out attacks on the Germans. Once the Germans were forced out of the trenches, the Allies could push them back. Pershing's troops were trained to fight a mobile war.

THE AMERICAN EXPEDITIONARY FORCE

French and British forces were exhausted by the time American troops arrived in France. They had been fighting in the trenches for three years. By that time, Russia was barely in the war. Italy was struggling against Austria-Hungary. Germany's U-boats had become a serious threat. The Americans seemed to be the only hope for the Allies.

Months after the U.S. had declared war on Germany, the AEF finally arrived in Europe. The Allies expected that their troubles would be over. The American soldiers were healthy and eager to fight. However, they were not the army that the Allies had hoped for.

Major Events
1917

April 6
America declares war on Germany.

May
John Pershing is given command of the AEF.

June 26
First U.S. troops arrive in France.

> Disembarked at 7:45 A.M.– K. Co. finest troops to land on French Soil. Welcomed very pleasantly. Children along roads asked for pennies, women threw flowers from balconies on to us.
>
> ENTRY OF JUNE 26TH, 1917 FROM THE DIARY OF CPT. FRANCIS M. VAN NATTER, CO. G, 28TH INFANTRY

TRANSPORTING THE TROOPS

The U.S. Navy was quickly building new ships, but there were not enough to transport men and supplies. Many troops were sent on British ships. The U.S. also took over any German ships in their ports. To protect the troops from U-boats, the ships traveled in groups, or convoys, with naval vessels.

The trip from New York to France took about 12 days. Many of the ships were so crowded that soldiers had to take turns sleeping. The food was terrible, and many men got seasick.

JOHN J. PERSHING
(1860–1948)

The First Arrivals

In June 1917, the first Americans arrived. There were only 14,000 men, and half of those had very little training or discipline. Many of the men were uneducated, and others didn't speak English. Few had ever used a rifle or any other weapon. They could barely march in step.

The first American arrivals trained with Allied troops. They also relied on the Allies for transportation and many supplies. U.S. soldiers usually traveled to Europe on British ships. They fired weapons that came from Allied factories. In 1917, American soldiers even had trouble getting warm coats and feed for pack animals.

An Independent Army

The Allies wanted to use American troops to replace French and British men who had been lost in battle. This would

"Black Jack" Pershing grew up on a farm and started his career as a teacher. To get a better education, he took an exam to go to the military academy at West Point. After graduating in 1886, he spent a number of years out West, fighting Native Americans.

Pershing served in both Cuba and the Philippines during the Spanish-American War. In 1906, President Theodore Roosevelt promoted him to general—the youngest in the army. When World War I began, Pershing was in Mexico, trying to end troubles there. He was called back to the U.S. in 1917 to lead the AEF.

split up the U.S. force between Allied armies. Pershing was willing to work with Britain and France, but he didn't want his men to serve under them. He wanted a united, independent American army under his command.

At the end of 1917, there were still only about 100,000 AEF soldiers in Europe. There were about 325,000 by March 1918. By that summer, over one million Americans were ready for action. General Pershing's independent army was finally taking shape.

THE FIRST SHOTS

The first AEF soldiers arrived in Europe in May–June 1917. The troops saw action in France on the Western Front. In October 1917, an American unit was sent to the trenches near the Swiss border. The French and Germans there had not fought each other since the beginning of the war. Sometimes the two armies fired artillery shells at each other, but the shells landed harmlessly.

When the Americans arrived, they were eager to fight. When a soldier fired the first AEF artillery shell of the war, it hit the German trenches. A few days later, the Germans struck back. They blasted the U.S. troops with artillery, then attacked. Two American soldiers were killed—the first of the AEF forces to die in the war. The deaths made the war real for Americans at home. For the American soldiers, this small skirmish introduced the horrors of trench warfare.

ABOVE: *American soldiers move carefully through barbed wire as they emerge from their trench*

CHAPTER 4

THE AEF ON THE WESTERN FRONT

In 1918, morale was low for both the Allies and the Central Powers. Millions of men had been killed or wounded, but trench warfare had made it impossible for either side to claim victory. At home, the warring nations were suffering terribly. Their citizens were starving, and their towns were destroyed. It looked like there was no end in sight.

AMERICANS IN THE TRENCHES

American soldiers were not trained in trench warfare, so new arrivals were often sent to quiet parts of the Western Front. There, they could get used to the terrible conditions that the Allied troops had experienced for years.

The trenches stretched for hundreds of miles (kilometers). They were surrounded by bleak, treeless land that was covered with barbed wire and pitted with shell holes. Soldiers slept and ate in the cramped, muddy passages that smelled like sewers. The men were plagued by diseases, as well as with lice and rats. At any time, soldiers might be torn apart by artillery or machine gun fire. Even in quiet zones, American were wounded and killed.

RIGHT: *American and French troops in the trenches along the Western Front*

Major Events
1918

May 28
Battle of Cantigny: first major battle using AEF and Allied forces

July 18
Battle of Château-Thierry: first action of AEF under Pershing

August 8
Battle of Amiens: end of trench warfare

September 12
Battle of Saint-Mihiel: Pershing commands AEF and French troops

November 11
Armistice is signed. The war ends.

THE LUDENDORFF OFFENSIVE

The Germans decided to make one last push. They wanted to smash the Allies before the Americans were able to help. The German commander General Erich Ludendorff planned to strike fast and attack with everything he had. Troops and weapons were brought in from the Eastern Front, where Russia was no longer a threat.

Ludendorff's first attack was against the French and British on March 21, 1918. The battle ended two weeks later, with many casualties on both sides. Germany had pushed back the British, but its army did not have the power or supplies to continue. The Allies knew, though, that they were in danger. To defeat Germany, they needed more American help.

> "... at times one's legs shake like a reed in the wind. It's a strange sensation when the shrapnel starts to drop all around you. Alarms of gas screaming all over the area, mud waist high... trenches not 4 feet deep and a gap wide between your **parapet** and Fritz's [German soldiers]. It sure is not a grand and glorious feeling. There's nothing you can conceive that can picture to your mind the condition of no man's land. It certainly was named correctly. ... Dead Germans. Equipment, legs, wine stink, mud, water holes and more holes, and oh my the barbed wire.
>
> **LETTER OF MARCH 19TH, 1918 FROM 1ST LT. DANIEL J. BIRMINGHAM**

Allied leaders urged President Wilson to send more troops quickly. They still wanted to use American soldiers in their own armies, but General Pershing would not agree. Finally, it was decided that the Americans would form their own army, but it would be under the control of French General Ferdinand Foch, the commander of all Allied action.

WHAT DO YOU THINK?
Why did the Germans decide to launch the Ludendorff Offensive?

The AEF's First Combat

On April 9, Ludendorff moved against the British. He planned to divide the French and British by forcing the British army toward the English Channel. The British had to protect the ports where they got their supplies. Despite tremendous losses, they managed to hold off the German attack.

The AEF was supporting the French army. On April 20, they took part in their first full-scale battle in France. American troops occupied an area near an abandoned village called Seicheprey. They were caught by surprise when 3,000 Germans raided the village. The small band of inexperienced doughboys was easily beaten back.

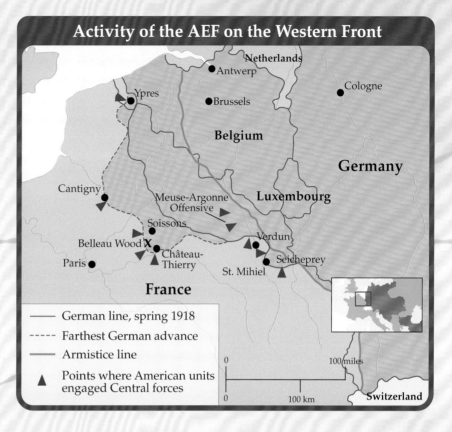

Activity of the AEF on the Western Front

— German line, spring 1918
---- Farthest German advance
— Armistice line
▲ Points where American units engaged Central forces

The next day, U.S. troops recaptured the village, but with many casualties. Germany used the incident for propaganda to show the superiority of German soldiers. General Pershing was upset that the first major action by the AEF made the Americans look incompetent.

WHAT DO YOU KNOW?

COMMUNICATIONS
One of General Pershing's biggest concerns was communication. It was hard for commanders to keep control because they were often far from the battlefield and the front lines extended for miles (kilometers). A number of methods were used to maintain contact. The fastest was by field telephones or telegraphs. Signal Corps soldiers would brave no man's land and the darkness to set up communication wires. Though slower, the simplest way was to send a runner with a handwritten note. One of the most effective methods was carrier pigeon. The army had 15,000 pigeons. A small patrol could easily carry a few pigeons in a basket to release when needed.

BELOW: *Field telephones were very basic, but they worked.*

The Third German Advance

On May 27, Ludendorff launched another huge attack. This time, German forces advanced to within 60 miles (97 km) of Paris. They also captured many supplies, weapons, and prisoners. Germany hoped France would give up before Paris was taken. Dispirited French troops began to retreat.

The Battle of Cantigny

The AEF was sent to capture the small village of Cantigny. It had an important observation post near railroad lines that carried German supplies. The Americans began the attack on May 28 in the early morning. Within three hours, U.S. troops had captured Cantigny. They then held off seven German **counterattacks**.

> " … these magnificent youths from overseas, … radiating strength and health … produced a great effect. They contrasted strikingly with our regiments in their faded uniforms, wasted by so many years of war…. We had the impression that we were about to see a wonderful transfusion of blood. Life was coming in floods to reanimate the dying body of France.
>
> **A FRENCH OFFICER DESCRIBING THE EFFECT OF THE AMERICAN INFANTRY** "

Pershing was thrilled. The stain of the American loss in Seicheprey had been removed. The battle was not a major victory, but it boosted American morale. The healthy, spirited young Americans also gave hope to the tired Allied troops. Pershing changed his mind about keeping his army separate from the Allies. He offered them all of the AEF's resources.

The Battle of Belleau Wood

General Foch, the French commander, saw that the Germans were getting weak. He decided to attack them with a combined force of French and U.S. troops. The Americans were sent to a small area called Belleau Wood.

ABOVE: *U.S. Marine Corps Memorial, Belleau Wood, France*

Both marines and soldiers took part. It was the first time the U.S. had sent in such a large offensive force.

The German army had set up very strong defenses. Hills were ringed with barbed wire and machine guns. On June 6, the Americans attacked and were met by fierce German resistance. The U.S. marines moving forward in rows across the open field were torn apart by machine gun fire. When they reached enemy lines, men fought hand-to-hand and with bayonets. The bloody battle continued until June 26, when the Americans finally captured the area.

The French were moved by the bravery of the U.S. marines. They renamed the area "Marine Brigade Wood." The Americans also made a big impression on their enemies. The Germans had hoped to show that the AEF could not fight. They were proven wrong.

RIGHT: *Nurses tend to wounded French soldiers at a train station that was converted to a hospital.*

WHAT DO YOU KNOW?

MEDICAL CARE
Over 30,000 U.S. doctors served in the war. Many women volunteered as nurses through the Red Cross and 13,000 enlisted. Doctors and nurses worked long hours, often in cold and miserable conditions. They treated terrible wounds from machine guns and artillery shells, as well as infections, gas burns and poisoning, and shell shock. In 1918, many died treating patients during the flu epidemic.

Near the front, wounded soldiers were taken to portable hospitals that had tents, floors, cots, and medical equipment. Hotels, churches, and other buildings were converted into hospitals away from the battlefield.

THE TURNING POINT

General Ludendorff planned to make another large attack against the Allies near the Marne River. He didn't know that the French had already learned of his plans. On July 15, the Germans were about to fire their artillery. Suddenly French and American guns began **bombarding** the German-held positions.

The Second Battle of the Marne looked like it would be a German victory at first. The Germans had captured a lot of territory. Ludendorff put everything into this battle. If Germany didn't win, it would face terrible problems at home. Their countrymen had suffered greatly because of the war. A loss might lead to a **revolution**, like the one in Russia.

General Foch now had the support of American soldiers. He knew the Germans didn't have the strength to keep up their attack. The combined Allied and American forces launched a counterattack on July 18. In one of its first major offensives, the AEF attacked along with the French army near Château-Thierry and Soissons. The Germans were caught by surprise. After three days of fighting, the Allies pushed across the Marne River. They drove the Germans back to their original lines.

ABOVE: *American soldiers successfully drove the Germans out of Château-Thierry.*

The Second Battle of the Marne helped change the course of the war. France recaptured lost territory and villages. Germany retreated and was on the **defensive**. It had 168,000 casualties and lost many weapons and important supplies. It was the worst German defeat in four years.

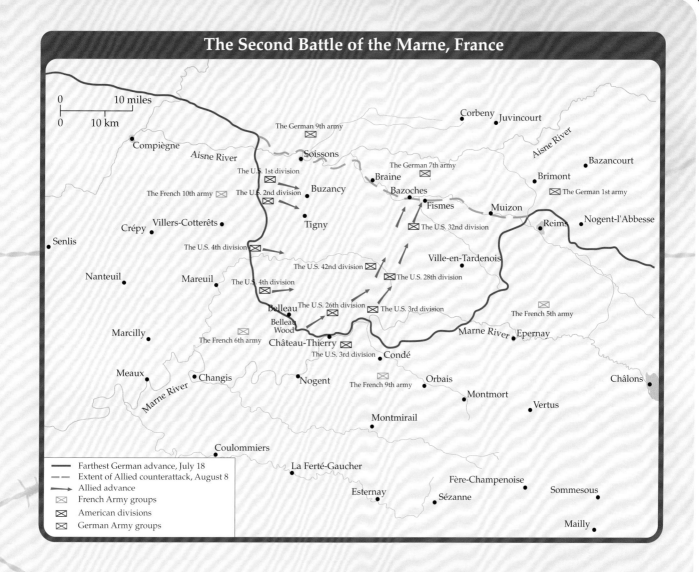

The Second Battle of the Marne, France

The Second Battle of the Marne in northeastern France marked the beginning of the end of the Great War. The victory was costly for the Allied forces. Nearly 95,000 French soldiers were either wounded or killed. About 85,000 American troops fought in the battle, and approximately 12,000 Americans were either killed or wounded. The battlefront was only about 60 miles (97 km) from Paris.

THE ALLIES GO ON THE OFFENSIVE

The German army was no longer the unstoppable force it had been. Many of its well-trained troops had been killed or wounded. They were replaced by very young or very old soldiers. Its men had lost the will to fight. In the meantime, more Americans arrived. By August, there were over a million AEF troops in France.

On August 8, the Allies and Americans began a new offensive with a surprise attack near the town of Amiens. They used hundreds of tanks and aircraft, as well as ground troops. They were no longer stuck in a defensive war.

The Germans were pushed back more. Foch wanted to continue the offensive. Neither France nor Britain had the resources to fight in every battle. It was time for the AEF to fight on its own. General Pershing named himself the commander of the U.S. First Army.

THE HARLEM HELLFIGHTERS

Many African-American soldiers were drafted, but they were often treated unfairly. Very few were allowed to become officers. Black troops usually were commanded by white officers. Many also served as laborers, rather than being formed into combat units.

New York's 369th Infantry became known as the Harlem Hellfighters because of their impressive reputation in combat. The Hellfighters were sent to France in December 1917, where they served with the French throughout the war. They spent more time on the front than any American unit, and the entire regiment received the French Croix de Guerre, or War Cross, for bravery.

LEFT: *New York's 369th Infantry was the AEF's first all black regiment. Their success on the battlefield left a mark on the AEF and helped to change America's opinion of the African-American soldier.*

U.S. WAR IN THE AIR

The Wright brothers made the first successful airplane flight only 10 years before the war began. By the end of the war, the airplane had become an important military weapon.

Development of War Planes

The Wright brothers developed one of the first military airplanes in 1909. However, in 1914, no one was quite sure how to use airplanes in battle. The planes could not fly far or fast. They were also fragile. At first, planes had the same function as observation balloons. They flew above enemy lines to gather information about troop movements and weapon placement.

As the war went on, planes became faster, sturdier, and more powerful. Instead of just observing targets below, they started bombing them. Bombs were invented for air attacks, and planes were fitted with bomb racks. Machine guns were designed to shoot through spinning propellers. This allowed the pilot to engage in "dogfights," or air battles with enemy pilots. They could also fire at targets on the ground.

ABOVE: *The 1909 Wright Military Flyer was the world's first military airplane.*

The American Air Service

At the start of the war, none of the main warring nations had many aircraft. Soon, though, both Allied and German factories were producing thousands of planes. When the U.S. joined the war, it had only 55 airplanes and none were ready for fighting. America agreed to provide thousands of planes and pilots by 1918. Unfortunately, only 417 American planes ever made it to the Western Front. U.S. pilots usually flew British or French fighters.

The American Air Services did not become a separate branch of the armed forces until March 1918. Training for American pilots took place in a U.S. flying school in France. In September 1917, the first pilots to arrive were the 200 men of the 26th Aero Squadron.

After learning basic skills, most American pilots continued to train at French schools. Some went to British and Italian schools. The British also trained thousands of aircraft mechanics. By the final months of the war, there were 45 U.S. squadrons at the front. They fought in only a few major battles, but still shot down almost 900 enemy planes and balloons, and dropped 140 tons (127 tonnes) of bombs.

> [We] thought that we were introducing into the world an invention which would make further wars practically impossible.
>
> **ORVILLE WRIGHT ABOUT THE AIRPLANE**

EDDIE RICKENBACKER
(1890–1973)

An "ace" was a pilot who shot down five enemy planes. Eddie Rickenbacker shot down 26 and was called the "ace of aces." His flying feats at St. Mihiel and Meuse-Argonne made him famous.

Rickenbacker came from a German-American family. He was a well-known race-car driver in the United States. In March 1918, he joined the American Air Service. By May, he had shot down his fifth plane.

After the war, he left the service. He enjoyed an exciting life and a long career as an airline executive.

ABOVE: *American soldiers fought fiercely under heavy enemy fire in the forest near St. Mihiel.*

The Battle of Saint-Mihiel

The Americans' first solo action was at St. Mihiel. The Germans had controlled this area for four years. It guarded an important railroad line. On September 12, Pershing began his attack. For four hours, over a million artillery and poison gas shells were fired. When the soldiers finally advanced, there was little resistance from the Germans.

The fighting on the ground was supported by an air attack. Almost 1,500 Allied planes took part. The new American Air Services had 609 pilots. It was the first time so much air power had ever been used. The Germans had fewer than 300 airplanes.

The pilots dropped bombs and fired machine guns while troops and tanks fought below. It took only two days for the U.S. First Army to capture the area, along with thousands of prisoners and hundreds of artillery guns.

The Battle of Meuse-Argonne

General Foch knew he had the upper hand. The Allies needed to quickly launch an all-out attack to smash the German army. This final major offensive lasted from September 26 until the end of the war.

American troops were assigned to clear the Argonne Forest near the Meuse River. It was an important area for the Germans because the railroad there brought in supplies. Pershing had two weeks to move his army 50 miles (80 km) after fighting ended in St. Mihiel. Over 600,000 weary men had to travel over muddy roads in the dark of night. There were also thousands of trucks, tanks, animals, and supply wagons that got stuck in the thick mud.

When the Americans arrived, they found an area with many hills and dense woods. The Germans had been there since 1914 and had built strong defenses. U.S. soldiers faced a tough fight against a well-placed network of trenches, machine guns, and artillery. American troops made progress at first. Soon, though, the difficult landscape led to brutal battles.

WHAT DO YOU KNOW?

THE LOST BATTALION

On October 2, nearly 600 U.S. troops found themselves surrounded by Germans in the Argonne forest. They could not get back to American lines. The next day, the Americans started firing shells into that area, not knowing that their own men were there. The only way the "Lost Battalion" could communicate with their army was by pigeon. One bird remained out of the original six. When a message was tied to his leg, he flew right onto a tree and wouldn't budge. At last, he flew off, but the men had little hope that he would survive. The bird lost an eye and a leg, but he made it to headquarters. The Lost Battalion was rescued five days later.

The fighting continued throughout October with terrible losses for both sides. In November, the Americans broke through the German defenses. At the same time, British and Belgian troops had also pushed the Germans back. By this time, they had broken through the Hindenburg Line, Germany's main line of fortified defenses along the Western Front. The mighty German army was on the run.

LEFT: *American soldiers covered their ears during the bombardment of German military positions.*

PEACE AT LAST

Even before the final battle began in Argonne, the Germans had sent a telegram to President Wilson. They wanted to make a peace settlement, or armistice, with the Americans. They were afraid that Britain and France would want harsher terms. President Wilson and the Germans negotiated for weeks, but they could not reach an agreement.

At last, when the German government could wait no longer, they set up a meeting with the French and British. The German people no longer supported the war. There were uprisings by the navy and army. On November 9, Germany's ruler, the kaiser, fled the country.

The Allies asked Germany to immediately leave all the territory it had captured and return all Allied prisoners. It also had to turn over all its weapon and war materials, as well as submarines. France and England wanted to make sure Germany could not rebuild its army.

On November 11, 1918, Germany agreed to the peace terms. At 11:00 that morning, the armistice went into effect. The fighting ended at the 11th hour on the 11th day of the 11th month. In June 1919, the Treaty of Versailles was signed by the warring nations, officially ending World War I.

> " When the firing ceased all along the front line it… was so quiet it made me feel as if I'd been suddenly deprived of my ability to hear. "
>
> **A SOLDIER AFTER THE ARMISTICE WENT INTO EFFECT AT 11:00 A.M.**

AMERICA'S CONTRIBUTIONS TO THE ALLIED VICTORY

When America entered the war, it barely had an army. Its factories could not produce the equipment that it needed to fight. Germany did not believe that the Americans would be much of a threat, and the Allies worried that American troops would not be prepared. The U.S. army proved them both wrong.

In 19 months of war, America raised a force of nearly four million men. Industries quickly started producing food and war materials for both their own men and the Allies. Even though the AEF saw only five months of combat, it made a great difference to the exhausted French and British. With the help of the AEF, the Allies were finally able to move out of the trenches and mount a strong offensive.

43

The United States was now the world's major power. The bloody, costly war had ruined the economies and populations of France, Britain, and Germany. There was political unrest everywhere. The Germans, in particular, were disgusted by the war's outcome. Although the war was over, the destruction left bitter wounds. The Treaty of Versailles would not bring lasting peace.

BELOW: *American soldiers at Armistice Day parade, November 11, 1918, Paris, France*

" A few nights ago the good news reached us that hostilities had ceased and it was a great occasion. Bands played, thousands of people with flags paraded around, women wept and men embraced each other like children. Poor France after her 4 years of mourning just broke. We are not speculating on when we are starting for home. Ah, that will be the time. And when we arrive in New York that will be some day. "

LETTER OF NOVEMBER 13TH, 1918 FROM 1ST LT. DANIEL J. BIRMINGHAM, 28TH INF., CO. M

FURTHER READING AND WEBSITES

BOOKS

Berg, A. Scott. *Wilson*. New York: Putnam, 2013.

Boghardt, Thomas. *The Zimmermann Telegram: Intelligence, Diplomacy, and America's Entry into World War I.* Annapolis: Naval Institute Press, 2012.

Doenecke, Justus D. *Nothing Less Than War: A New History of America's Entry into World War I (Studies in Conflict, Diplomacy and Peace).* Lexington: University of Kentucky Press, 2011.

Hemingway, Ernest. *A Farewell To Arms.* New York: Simon and Schuster, 1995.

Keene, Jennifer D. *World War I: The American Soldier Experience.* Winnipeg: Bison Books, 2011.

Machen, Gresham and J. Gresham Machen. *Letters from the Front: J. Gresham Machen's Correspondence from World War 1.* Phillipsburg: R&R Publishing, 2012.

Remarque, Erich Maria and A.W. Wheen. *All Quiet on the Western Front.* New York: Fawcett Books, 1987.

Rubin, Richard. *The Last of the Doughboys: The Forgotten Generation and Their Forgotten World War.* New York: Houghton Mifflin Harcourt, 2013.

Vaughn, David K. *Letters from a War Bird: The World War I Correspondence of Elliot White Springs.* Columbia: University of South Carolina Press, 2012.

Bausum, Ann. *Unraveling Freedom: The Battle for Democracy on the Home Front During World War I.* Washington, D.C.: National Geographic Children's Books, 2010.

WEBSITES

Hemingway on War and Its Aftermath
www.archives.gov/publications/ prologue/2006/spring/ hemingway.html

World War I Selective Service System Draft Registration Cards, M1509
www.archives.gov/research/military/ ww1/draft-registration/

Commemorating the Great War
www.worldwar-1centennial.org/index. php/history/why-commemorate.html

MILESTONES: 1914–1920, American Entry into World War I, 1917
www.history.state.gov/milestones/ 1914–1920/wwi

GLOSSARY

adobe	sun-dried bricks made of clay or mud and straw
alliances	formal associations of nations or groups
armistice	an agreement to stop fighting a war
assassinated	murdered by surprise attack, often for political reasons
blockade	to isolate or block a harbor to stop people or supplies from entering or leaving the country
bombarding	attacking with bombs, explosive shells, or missiles
bonds	certificates of debt issued by the government, which agrees to pay back the borrowed money plus interest
brutality	cruel and often violent treatment of other people
counterattacks	attacks by a defending force against an attacking enemy force to regain lost ground
defensive	enduring or preventing attack
demonstrations	events in which people gather together to show their support or opposition to a person or issue
disputes	arguments; quarrels
draft	to select people for a special purpose, usually service in the armed forces
exaggerated	enlarged or increased beyond the normal
harassed	tormented; attacked repeatedly
immigrants	people who come to a country to take up permanent residence
inhuman	merciless, cruel, and lacking in empathy
lottery	a system where chance is used to decide who will get or be given something
manufacturing	making from raw materials, usually with machines in factories
martyr	someone who chooses to die for a specific reason or cause
merchant	having to do with the buying and selling of goods; one who engages in trade
modified	changed for a specific purpose
munitions	war materials including weapons and ammunition

neutral	not aligned with or supporting a side in a war, dispute, or contest
pacifist	one who is strongly and actively opposed to conflict and war
parapet	a low wall or embankment designed to protect soldiers from enemy fire
propaganda	ideas, information, or rumors spread for the purpose of helping or hurting an organization, issue, or person
recession	a period of economic activity that has undergone a downward turn
recruits	new members of the armed forces
refrained	held oneself back; chose another course of action
refugees	people who flee to a foreign country or power in search of safety or protection
register	a system for or act of selecting individuals from a group (as for compulsory military service)
revolution	the usually violent overthrow of one government to start a new one
rural	of or pertaining to the country, country people, country life, or agriculture
slogan	a word or phrase used to express a characteristic position or to attract attention
stalemate	a situation in which further action is blocked; a deadlock
telegram	a message by telegraph
unrestricted	having no limitations; not confined or reserved to a certain area
urban	of or pertaining to the city, city people, or city life
Victory bread	bread made with substitutes for wheat flour, such as corn, rye, or potato flour

INDEX